Another Kind of Travel

Phoenix Poets
A Series Edited by Robert von Hallberg

Another Kind of Travel
Paul Lake

For Michael McFee with admiration and best wishes

Paul Lake

Nov. 13, 1992

The University of Chicago Press
Chicago and London

Paul Lake is associate professor of English and creative writing at
Arkansas Tech University. His poetry has appeared in two chapbooks,
Bull Dancing and *Catches*, and numerous publications including *The
New Republic, The American Scholar,* and *Partisan Review.*

The University of Chicago Press, Chicago 60637
The University of Chicago Press, Ltd., London

Library of Congress Cataloging-in-Publication Data
Lake, Paul, 1951–
    Another kind of travel.

    (Phoenix poets)
I. Title. II. Series.
PS3562.A379.A8   1988   811'.54   87-14705
ISBN 0-226-46807-0
ISBN 0-226-46808-9 (pbk.)

For Tina

Some of these poems appeared in the following magazines:
The American Scholar. "Blue Jay"
California Quarterly. "An Apparition"
Cumberland Poetry Review. "Catches," "A Change of Scene"
Inquiry. "Hypochondriac"
Island Magazine (Australia). "Lost Driving in the Ozarks"
Ironwood. "Pelican"
Maryland Poetry Review. "The Heart of Darkness"
Nebo. "The Toltec Mounds"
The New Republic. "In Rough Weather"
Occident. "Crossing America by Bus," "A Dieter," "Summer
    Revisited"
Partisan Review. "The Age of Terror"
Pequod. "While Watching the *Ballet folklórico nacional de
    Mexico*"
Poetry Australia. "Summer Revisited"
Poetry Northwest. "Concerning Angels: A Poetry Reading"
Poetry Now. "Summer"
The Reaper. "Hog Killing Christmas"
Southwest Review. "The Rooster"
Texas Review. "Introduction to Poetry"
Threepenny Review. "An American in Paris," "The Boat,"
    "Crime and Punishment," "Lost Driving in the Ozarks,"
    "South of the City"

In addition, "Hypochondriac" appeared in the 1985 edition of
*The Anthology of Magazine Verse and Yearbook of American
Poetry,* published by Monitor Book Company. "South of the
City," "Crime and Punishment," "The Age of Terror," "Blue
Jay," "In Rough Weather," "Catches," and "Introduction to
Poetry" appeared in a limited edition chapbook entitled
Catches, published by R. L. Barth in 1986.

A special thanks to Wendy Lesser, editor of the *Threepenny
Review,* who has published such a large number of my poems
and reviews over the last several years.

Contents

Part One: The Age of Terror

The Heart of Darkness

First day of school,
I'm late, as usual,
running to class when
I find I'm once again
rounding a corridor,
                    then up a stair
to homeroom
(that euphemism)
in the familiar nightmare—
life in a Baltimore ghetto junior high.

Checking my schedule,
there are one, two, three, four, five
periods in a row with no relief.
Policing classroom and hall,
I shout perpetually above a chorus
of raucous adolescent voices
until, my voice grown hoarse,
I'm tired and shaken
from stopping fistfights, confiscating weapons
and sifting through the wreckage of the day
for torn out pages
to stick back with tape.

I'm tired, I'm tired

of watching, as fleet-footed Donna Henson
waltzes on tiptoe like a boxing champ
into a hopeless future,
                        as Clarence Brown
grows surlier as my every well-intentioned
effort to quell the noise and simply teach
falls flat, when someone throws a book or punch
or upends a desk,
filling the room with thunder
hard as anger.

Easy now to feel relief
next to my wife in bed
a decade later.
The nightmare ended, I can mutter now
like Conrad's Kurtz, *The horror!*
                        Yes, the horror—

Not of my short two-year commute
into the heart of darkness, but
of those mean streets I'd visit after work
where a generation grows up fatherless
in violence and squalor
and where nearly one in twenty
men's lives will be cut short
in bloody nightmare—

in Wilmington, Baltimore, Oakland, Newark, New York—

the blight at the swollen heart of the American city.

South of the City

Where a rag of flame flaps over a gas pipe,
the one token of color
   in the gray mélange,
                      and the sky hangs
like a sheet of corrugated iron
   from the tips of cranes

above scrap mountains, these gray, fog-colored men
move through an iron thicket,
   pruning with blow-torches
                      the barbed tendrils
of wire, cutting and rooting up the rust-brown
   unblooming flowers

of metal, petal and stem. Like gardeners
of the inanimate, they
   harrow the gray detritus,
                      plow with forklift,
derrick, and bulldozer the tangled scrap piles
   the rain unsilvers.

Bed springs, sheet metal, engine blocks, the three-tiered
car lot of abandoned wrecks
   await election
                    in the steel jaws'
glowering descent, the foundry's purgatory,
   and transfiguration,

while these men squat next to the makeshift dolmen
of crushed cars in a junk-lot
     Stonehenge. Fugitive
                         from architecture,
these featureless, sheet metal buildings, open
     on one side to air

through which no iron deliverer descends
into the godforsaken
     landscape, where black
                         stacks of abandoned
car batteries wait next to rusting freight cars
     idle on side rails,

their acids draining
into the neutral ground.

A Dieter

Shape-shifter, self-transformer,
whose face is that face in the glass,
round and fat as a pumpkin,
her hand like a banana bunch,
her breasts plump melons?
Year after year, I kill her,
but she grows back like a crop.
We're like those identical twins
named Before and After, each
at her end of the telescope.

Seven fat sleek cows climbed up out of a river
to graze on reeds, and, after them, seven gaunt, lean cows;
the gaunt cows ate the fat cows like a good supper,
but stayed rail thin.
                    That's a dieter's parable.

And Denial is a kind of religion
with its icons and saints—
the high-cheekboned model glaring from the magazine cover,
the martyr burning on her pyre
                    of anorexia nervosa.
                                        I know
what the glutton and the monk both know:
that the stomach, too, is a sexual organ
with many chords. I've played them all—
from the low, tremulous bass notes of a pendant belly
to the hysteric piano clink of starvation's upper register.

Now, as I turn to face my ugly sister,
she sucks in her cheeks
and puts on hunger
like a bad habit.

It hurts me to see her change
just when we were getting close.

Joined however we turn,
we are in this together
for better or worse
like a bad marriage. My Siamese twin,
we are stuck with each other.

Hypochondriac

I've gotten down the warning signs by heart,
                                    and every day
I check my body for some tell-tale change
confirming my gut feeling—
                    that I'm ill.
As if, when I intoned my litany
of cramps and aches, blackouts and fainting spells,
I could convince the doubting Thomases
that something terminal
is here, just out of sight, beneath my skin,
spreading its province, like some awful stain.

I note each transformation:
                    See this mole?
I'm sure now that it's darker than last year.
My ankles swell. And when I lift my tongue—
does all that purple pulp look *natural?*

No, the body will betray us. Sooner or later
a rise in temperature, or falling hair
will signal, like a flag, our own decline—
till on a sickbed or an operating table
we clutch our fists, pierced by the surgeon's lance,
our spirit, like our body, crucified.

And so I brace myself, I face the worst.
Because we're *bound* to suffer, and if it's done
in the right spirit—as if disease were normal,
and life and health unexpected miracles—
then any day without disease or pain
is almost heavenly.

                    Waking alone sometimes,
I'll see my death's head mirrored on the wall
across the room, and, pulling my covers back,
I'll pretend this robe's a white hospital gown,
the voices on the radio down the hall
the voices of other patients on my wing
where the hopeless cases wait . . .
                              and suddenly,
the light in the room, the laughter of my children
will swell around me like a cresting wave
until I'm staggered—merely to be living!
As if, while wandering between two worlds
I'd stumbled blinking into light,
or heard a kind voice say, "Case in remission. . . ."

Crime and Punishment
for Randy Rhoda

I close the book on *Crime and Punishment*
And think of you, my friend, the gifted student,
Who switched your major, once at M.I.T.,
To history, then anthropology—
Through half the catalogue in seven years,
First in, then out of school, grinding your gears.
Playing Raskolnikov, your plight became
Almost a joke between us. Now that name
Reminds me how the spiralling depression
That dragged you from confusion to confession
Blunted your gifts.
              For fourteen years of hard time
You stalked through Boston, but your only crime
Was killing your own future, spinning wheels
From Cambridge to the Back Bay's cobbled hills
Driving a taxi—or on all-night walks
Roaming the back streets, where, for several blocks,
You fled, one cold night, pounding the cement
Past stop sign, parked car, light, and tenement,
While steadily behind, a shadow gained,
Waving a pistol. When at last you turned
To face your nemesis, you met no double,
But a common thief, who cursed you for your trouble,
Rifling your wallet with, "What *is* this shit?
Just some goddamned IDs—go on, then, keep it,"
Then tossing back your life.

So what's your crime?
What spins you down the sidewalk like a dime
Wobbling, wobbling . . . always just off-center
As autumn passes and approaching winter
Makes Boston your Siberia, your fate
The tragedy you lived to recreate
For me each summer, turning your life to art,
While I, who should have been your counterpart,
Kept both at a safe distance, and now write
What you said then with such criminal delight.

The Age of Terror

No thunder across the steppes, no horde of Huns—
The rat-tat-tat of automatic guns
Rattles our quiet. On a downtown street
Of any capital where four roads meet
A statesman lies sprawled out on the crossroads—
Or turns a key: his limousine explodes,
And footfalls echo down the corridor
Of history, where no ambassador
Or minicam can follow.
                                    Blow your horn,
Roland or Gabriel, there's none to warn
Who hasn't seen already on TV
Some minister of ideology
Proclaim that as the sun sinks in the West
No Joshua can stall, no word arrest
The earth's sure revolutions at a command.
Instead, a darkness creeps across the land;
And since it's easier to turn toward night,
To bomb a power plant, than to shed light,
The sun fails in the West. A new Dark Age
Is ushered in as nations hemorrhage
At every severed artery where bands
Of ragtag soldiers issue their demands
At gunpoint. See, a new imperium
Broadcast by headline and by letter bomb
Replaces our old government of men. . . .

Until, by fiat, light's declared again
At midnight, and an iron rule replaces
The old chaos with universal stasis.
O brave new world! more catholic than Rome—
The sky spreads like a cupola or dome
Over the earth—wide, wider—till the last
Protestant voice is silenced in the vast
Inhuman northern cold, across whose snows
The far-flung stars are archipelagoes.

While Watching the Ballet folklórico nacional de Mexico

I
A black mat taped across the free-throw line
muffles their steps,
the feathers and flowers are crêpe,
and when the dancers whirl, step,
clatter their boot heels, toe-tap,
or slap the strings of their over-sized guitars,
polite applause
patters like falling rain. The thud of wet tennis balls
is all their feet can hammer from the matted floor.

II
Just so, just so.
                    In Montezuma's dream,
his shadow swept, a scythe across the ground,
and the Aztecs fell in windrows, as beneath
his black man-high wing span
their bodies passed—
                    until Cortez and Spain,
blood, gold, and all his dream forewarned
had come to pass. Preserved now in tapping feet,
the nightmare's simply called "The Feather Dance."

15

III
Parrot and peacock,
                    toucan, *Quetzal,* macaw—
all fade to colored ribbons, wadded rags,
and papier mâché, as, whirling their swords,
the *mestizo* dancers sidestep history,
slapping their thighs and clapping blades and spurs,
until a dance stepped by conquistadores
is lost in the spin, twirl, strike, and shout;
redubbed "The Spurs," its Christians and Infidels
were so much plumage to wide native eyes—
its strut and pomp of brass and drums and pipes,
birds chittering in branches or
                    a hubbub of peacocks.

IV
And other strange transplantings: Scottish jigs,
mazurkas, polkas, but for the program notes
would seem like jungle flowers, they're so transformed.
The dancers spin, and as their measures change,
the motley's gathered into one homespun
where folk are stitched to folk—their artless art
making the world a common stamping ground,
or a dark stage where distinctions are stamped out.

Now a lone dancer, wearing a stuffed deer's head
enters the spotlight. His right forepaw raised,
he mimics the high step and half-cocked ears
of wildness, as it whiffs the scent of man.
Another dancer stalks him, step for step,
till the drama's played out to its foregone end.

16

But for a moment we are breathless—
                              in the dark,
teased past the flickering shadows by bright lines
of bison and elk and staggering elephant,
which, pierced by phantom arrows, fall and die
forever, in a deathless plenitude;
where, after its throes, each victim walks again—
mammoth with man, and elk, and sabertooth.

Pelican

Past bombsites past bunkers the wind
hot   At the top of the stairs
in a room marked Top Secret we enter
banalities maps blackboards chairs

We say here's where I work here's the key
(they are waiting for us back at the house)
We enter without clearance here now
is the cot where I sleep now here
are the weights that I lift in off hours

Across deserts and deserts and deserts

On under near over the Bay

On a deck where a pelican circles
slowly beak bowed like a cargo plane
slowly slowly among gulls as in German
Polish English Look look a pelican look
till a gull culls him from the flock
        Across the deck   no other word

On under near over the Bay
In the rush hour traffic on Market

Or rising from the dark underworld
to the gray light as we enter West Oakland

A voice translates another voice prods
Sing goddess of the destructive wrath
That's of Peleus' son divine Achilles
who sent many brave warriors to hell
(in the gray light) and made countless bodies
prey for dogs (we reenter the tunnel)
and feasts for all manner of birds

San Francisco Alameda Berkeley Oakland
sway dance as when I watched coral reefs
in time-lapse surrender ossify

sway wavering behind the dark glass
like marine life   naval base   suburb   city

sitting elbow to elbow to elbow
riding north weary solitary
on the rumbling Greyhound thinking
dreaming through the moving window—

    Of all the earth

       my kind

    Of all my kind

       myself

Doglike so me and mine
are marked with a name a smell

sister niece brother friend sister friend
wife mother-in-law father-in-law

around our arms and around our necks

O open that narrowing swirl

Fall like the pelican
I saw on film today
after the awful scuttling
of claw tentacle and fang
in the crowded living room
weary from van bus taxi subway ferry

Falling gliding through the air
it was gone
alone suddenly beneath its clean splash

then unfolding appearing again
black wet a quivering fish

still alive in its splendid beak

O sudden lightning fall

on every hand eye fin bird bush

Blue Jay

A sound like a rusty pump beneath our window
Woke us at dawn. Drawing the curtains back,
We saw—through milky light, above the doghouse—
A blue jay lecturing a neighbor's cat
So fiercely that, at first, it seemed to wonder
When birds forgot the diplomacy of flight
And met, instead, each charge with a wild swoop,
Metallic cry, and angry thrust of beak.

Later, we found the reason. Near the fence
Among the flowerless stalks of daffodils,
A weak piping of feathers. Too late now to go back
To nest again among the sheltering leaves.
And so, harrying the dog, routing the cat,
And taking sole possession of the yard,
The mother swooped all morning.

                              I found her there
Still fluttering round my head, still scattering
The troops of blackbirds, head cocked toward my car
As if it were some lurid animal,
When I returned from work. Still keeping faith.
As if what I had found by afternoon
Silent and still and hidden in tall grass
Might rise again above the fallen world;
As if the dead were not past mothering.

Part Two: Heartland

In Rough Weather
for Steve

The storm blew up so suddenly,
cresting the hills, we just had time
to leave our hooks where they had caught
on the first cast, quickly cutting lines
and aiming our prow across the lake
to race the storm. Crouched in the hull,
I shouted directions while you fought,
with stuttering engine, swell after swell,
nosing our wave-clapped, drunken prow
into the whitecaps till it rang
or sipped at water in the troughs,
bellying to light. You timed each plunge
and kept us edging toward the shore
by starts—and when we took on water
and seemed, mid-lake, to stand stock-still,
you played big brother to your big brother,
steadying me with your steady skill.
And once, when we both thought we would flounder
and I looked back, we saw our fear
doubled by all that might go under—
and all that was dear was doubly dear.

Catches

As the sun sets, cast and reel,
cast and reel. As daylight falls,
and fishes' fins and dipping gulls
catch fire, drop your hook and feel,
tugging on your line's end, what's
elusive as an afterthought.

Minnows, and not leviathans,
ruffle the surface of these pools
and tug at worms; fierce snapping turtles
grip your hook till the rod bends,
and still you repeat your cast, and reel . . .
as if each promise made a meal.

The Rooster

This wasn't country, but a country town—
Our house, not two blocks distant from Main Street,
So when I heard the unaccountable, loud,
And not-too-distant crowing of a rooster,
I lay there almost more curious than annoyed
In the dark room, and when I couldn't sleep,
Got up, got dressed, then stood beside the window
As the sun rose and the early morning traffic
Hummed up and down the highway, north and south.

Sun glittered on the grass. It was early April.
Breath came in clouds as I stood on the front steps,
Cold startling my lungs, and every sudden cock crow
Against the newborn day echoing like brass.

Then, block by block, across the well-trimmed lawns
The manic cries moved closer, then withdrew,
Moved closer, then—
                        What was it behind the fence?—
But a blood-combed, black-ruffed, yellow-legged game rooster
With his loud, unlawful cock-a-doodle-doo
(Pronounced as in a children's story book,
But loud as reveille), a roving bugle
Brassy as day, rousing the neighborhood.

That was the first night.
                        On that first long day,
I tracked his call, a cry among bird cries
In the first light, in the hours before work,
Then went to work, fresh from reconnaisance
In the grassy fields—Oh, I felt lyrical—
Glad as the world turned one long natural cycle.

But wakened every night at 3 a.m.
Four hours into sleep, and *kept* awake,
I'd hear the rooster strutting down the block
Inexorably, neck swollen like a trumpet
(Unless he stopped to bend and peck at birdseed),
And, throwing the covers back with a hoarse curse
And rubbing my eyes and wrestling on my coat,
I'd plunge into the cold, a stone or brick
Cocked in my hand to crack his bloody crown.
I crouched behind a bush like an assassin.

But rocks and BBs failed: He merely squawked
And fluttered when my tin can piercing gun
Pumped pellets at him. Hit by rocks, he'd skid
Halfway across the driveway, still upright
To skitter away, legs churning, after a pause—
The way cartoon mice run before they run.

So in the dark, fumbling a telephone,
I called the police (four times), the animal shelter,
And the mayor's office, later in the day,
Each office in its turn referring me
To the next (roosters, it seems, being no one's business),
Until my fifth call, when, to shut me up,
The police dispatched a car.

                                    Oh, happy day!
The six-foot tall, two hundred-pound policeman
Climbed slowly from the front seat, closed the door—
And locked his car keys in the purring cage.

And when, above an eight-foot high storm fence
(Me eyeing all the while his holstered gun),
He trapped the bird, at last—picking a stone
Out of the grass ("We don't hardly *shoot* nothing . . .")
And stunning it into silence—
                              from the dead,
The cock rose, ruffling feathers as he stood
On the far side of the fence, to walk away.

Now that he's gone, the town is quieter.
Above the empty parking lots downtown
The clock turns on its pole, flashing the time
To the Baptist Church, then, slowly turning west,
To the county courthouse and the savings bank,
Where the automatic teller never sleeps,

As from a tree top, fluttering in slow motion,
A rooster falls and falls, hitting the ground
At a dead run, and an irate, sleepy mayor,
Waving a broomstick, tells his son-in-law
To come down from the tree to the wet lawn,
And blue policemen trespass down the block
To gather at the curb, where blue lights flash,
To pry at doors and paw at tight-sealed windows,
As static cackles from each locked blue car.

Lost Driving in the Ozarks

Where mountains crowd the horizons,
a casual labyrinth
of heat-stunned roads, blind turns
where direction alters
by slow shifts, and we move
with a sidling motion
into the unposted unknown. . . .

Here we buck stones and fling gravel
where the road dips
and at each hill crest
chart a new course which unravels
as the vague and dimming gray
in the west spreads to
all quarters as we turn—

past houses, trailers, then shacks,
whose dark inhabitants
seem shag-bearded, mat-haired and cover-alled
uncustomed strangers
as they watch from a sunken porch, or grin
from a passing truck, as we both nose
out of the other's path.

Yet if approached, they might prove neighborly,
their twang and drawl,
like Ariadne's thread,
giving direction.
But the heart knocks
as the ruts deepen, as the mind whispers,
What if a tire blows,

or the engine stalls and sputters in a cloud
of dust? Hard-hooved, bull-headed fear
stamps, paws the air and
bellows, its hot-breathed bawl
echoing down the nerves as we foresee
the long walk through the dusk or dark
on a shoulderless road,

a door, and then the shuffling, nervous phone call
as we assert,
between Somewhere and Here,
without signs and names for help,
hopeful connections.
But as the thunderer at the heart
raises its dust cloud,

panting as we spin
down one more narrowing lane,
the light quickens: we strike hardtop,
signs, and after a few false starts,
plot our course, and head for home—
And there, settle our hearts with drink,
distraction, laughter, as

over that distant crest—
while time and custom dull
its echoing din—
night takes the first valley.

The Toltec Mounds

Now shrub-covered under their
hundred years' growth of timber, they
rise less visibly against the flat
alluvium of delta soil—brute

whiskery, lumpish things, now all but
stranded—here where the highways flatten out
beyond the last exits
to suburbs, beyond the neighboring airport's

incessant wish to transcend
this native lushness, the near-tropical heat;
the river given now to thick-leaved cypress
where its channel bent

and where now every year more vague
against its backwash, the earthworks mouldering
to outlines on a map
seem less-than-mythic

swollen middenheaps.
Not even Toltec, as our guidebook says.
Walking among them, feeling their silences
become our own, we think of how

last century they seemed
to awed Midwestern farmers, vestiges
of lost civilizations, wandering tribes
from Aztlan or Atlantis,

Carthage, Tyre . . .
From here to Georgia,
north to Illinois, south to the Gulf,
rising above the fields

to tame the wilderness.
We think of how, in 1541,
DeSoto must have seen them shimmering there
against the gilt horizon, like a mirage

of Seven Cities, at the bayou's mouth
or along a river's fork—huge
flat-topped pyramids—
as he stumbled past them up the Arkansas.

Mound Builders, we say now, as if explaining
how the names were lost—
how everywhere we sift
among the bits and shards for golden tablets

and magic spectacles, we always find,
instead of proofs or parchments,
painted beads,
a broken arrowhead,

a pot whose glyphs turn out, upon inspection,
to merely decorate the native clay.
A hollow in the ground,
a mound of earth

ten thousand footsoles tamped into a shape
ascending toward the sun,
time and again
returning to its foot, then, basket by basket,

hauling the earth behind them up the long slope.

Summer

A road of dirt and stone
lies half under trees' shade.

Dust curtains sun,
blights flower, dulls leaf sheen.

Heavy, heavy the scent
of honeysuckle, heavy as rain.

Its sweetness falls
honey-thick on sense.

It dampens the dust down.

The Boat

Sit down a minute. The roast is in the oven
And it will be an hour before the men
Come clattering and banging up the driveway
Loud with their talk of this year's ten-point buck
That tiptoed past their stands, just out of range.
You've done your best. . . . I guess you've been too patient. . . .
I'll do the talking now to hurry things—
Though what it is I hardly dare tell you,
Much less my Bill, who thinks my life began
When our two met, and runs beside his now,
Like tractor tires, that's how he'd likely say.
Best to begin by saying it right out:
My recent "troubles," as some would have them called,
They're . . .
                    nothing I can name. . . .
                                        I want to say
"A man I used to love," but when I hear it,
I only think that, if I met him now,
He'd seem a boy, about my Cindy's age
Or older—tanned, with short brown hair combed back
Under his hat—a wide-brimmed Panama
With a red band, that made me laugh so hard
When I saw it that he had to laugh himself—
A quiet, shy, intellectual Yankee boy
From Harvard, no less, here in Arkansas!
You look at me now and find it hard to imagine,
But I was younger then, and not so shy
That when we asked to use my Daddy's boat
He cocked his eye and thought before answering.
(It had a cabin small as a doll's house

And a child-sized bunk. . . . But we were children then.)
I wish now, when I wish for anything,
To have spent that day, instead, without the sailing.
But there are no insteads. I've learned that much
From piling one instead on top another,
Thinking how that day might have turned out different
If Jack, at our first thought of turning back,
Hadn't brushed his hand so lightly against my thigh
And left it there. . . .
                                    Or when the boat blew over
And righted again, not fifty yards from shore,
We'd swum the distance home and then gone back
With an outboard and a rope.

                                    Instead, we giggled.
I kicked my shoes off. Jack just smiled and smiled
And treaded water. Then I stripped my pants
And laughed, "Come on, you Yankee Puritan,
Get those clothes off. . . . You can keep the hat,"
And teased him till he got behind the mast
And flutter-kicked while I tugged from a rope
On the bowsprit. We pulled and kicked and pulled—
You could see the boat's deck three feet under water—
And paddled slowly toward the nearest shore,
Which seemed so close, at first, then seemed so distant.
We heard the people talking on the sand,
But refused their help, urging each other on
With jokes until our breath grew short. Then Jack,
Seeing a block of wood bob to the surface
From down below, reached out to haul it in
And let go of the mast.

                    The boat kept moving
Faster than I'd have guessed. When I looked back,
Jack smiled at me that tight-lipped Yankee smile—
Too nervous or shy or tired to ask for help—
And disappeared. I called, "Stop teasing, Jack,"
Smiling myself—then growing desperate,
Swam to where he went down and tried to dive. . . . .

He'd left his wet clothes on. I've tried to think
How he could smile, feeling himself go under—
But what can thinking mend? He's drowned. I'm here.
And there, our husbands clattering down the road
With the tailgate down and hungry for their supper
Will expect loud talk and smiles on their return;
Our children, like a barefoot, screaming tribe,
Will run to greet the truck, and everyone,
Not knowing by what misses we're brought here
Instead of somewhere else, or not at all,
Won't sense the lives they've missed, while I feel mine
Always below me, like a sunken deck,
Hauling its nightmare tonnage of dark water.

Hog Killing Christmas

Tubs, gloves, boots, blood, fat, hogs' heads, entrails,
the glass knob on the back door so greased and slippery
with hog fat, I turned and turned it on the top step with two hands
and couldn't make it open—
                              that was Christmas.
That was, after Daddy let us open our presents a week too early,
all that was left on that first morning to do
after breakfast—a dull, cold, dry December day
perfect for hog killing, just as Daddy'd called it
when they set out to the barn
booted and gloved, to do the slaughtering.

Later, it became a family ritual
and Christmas meant
ax helves and hogs hung
upside down by the hocks; it meant
watching, as year by year, I grew
almost old enough, old enough, then too old to
merely wait, loafing in the living room
while Rexanne, my older sister, read
from Tennyson's *Idylls of the King*
or "Break, break, break/On thy cold gray stones, O Sea,"
which I had given her one year
in a leather-bound book.

Always the bookworm,
always the baby. . . .
Even hunting I'd never killed bigger game
than squirrels or rabbits,
for most of my life content
to be my older sister's little brother,
in love with words, while always somewhere nearby
my brother and father performed their offices
for the farm and family,
blood drenched in the clamorous hog pen
or piling hay.

Imagine a boy
like that, my joy when,
after she'd married and moved away,
Rexanne came back, not many months afterwards
alone and uncharacteristically
quiet, to visit at Christmas time
and resume the old intimacy
of coconspirators
against the routine of the family farm.

At supper, the truth came out:
Divorced and bankrupt.

Eyes down (except to glance at me), she tried to explain:
"It's better this way, Daddy."

                    Then Daddy, uncomprehending:
"You don't want to pay your debts to the people you owe?"

"It's not like *that*."

"Well, what then?"

A long silence.
". . . We've sold the horses. All except that stallion
You gave—you loaned us—can't I please keep *that?*"

My chair whined as I pushed back from the table
and said in a voice which nearly frightened me,
"I guess I'm ready to help with the slaughtering now."

Then Daddy to me:
"We've finished the slaughtering, son. It's almost dark."

Then teary-eyed, I appealed to my brother Buddy:
"Well, what's left then? Isn't there anything?"

"Just one. That sow. The one you call Doreen."

I was out the door then, pulling on my snow boots
without a coat and heading toward the barn,
while in the dusk—quietly, hastily
putting on gloves and aprons even as they walked—
Buddy and Daddy crossed the dark behind me.

I grabbed an ax
and brought the blunt end down between the eyes
hard, before the sow could even flinch,
though for a half second
her look said, as her eyes met mine,
I Know.

41

Then Buddy called, "She's dead—
Daddy, bring the knife,"
and I lay the ax handle down.
                              We slit the throat
and Daddy knelt down beside us as she bled,
his movements slow, as if he moved in sleep
or underwater, bending to wet his hand
where the blood flowed—and then suddenly
drawing his warm wet hand across my face.

"What are you doing, Daddy?" Buddy looked surprised
when he saw my bloodied face.

                              "I'm marking him—
this hog here's his first kill."

                              But that's for hunting, Daddy,
that's for deer."

I thought I heard him mumble, "He ain't been hunting,"
as he stood up, like a bear or elephant
rousing himself from sleep, to turn toward the house.
Then he hunched toward the back porch, still sleepwalking,
to where a halo spread out from the light
on the frosty air, and, mounting the three steps,
entered the kitchen.

"The way he's done you, you think you'd killed a bear.
Go on . . ." Buddy smiled, ". . . I'll finish up myself."

By the time I got to the house, Daddy was sitting down
across from Rexanne, eating a slice of pie.
I pulled a chair up and sat down next to him
to cut a piece myself. Then happening
to look up when I heard the room go quiet,
I had to stare back twice to recognize
that the bloodied face against the stainless silver
of the toaster's warping side was my own face
startled to see, behind its mask of blood,
a face, my face—the face that I was born with.

Part Three: Travellers in Space and Time

A Change of Scene

If it's fields we're bound for, a voice whispers, "Fields,"
The earth is swept of wrinkles, like a bed.
And falling through the night air, trailing a sheet,
We compose ourselves to meet the new landscape
As we compose the features of the land
Ballooning toward us from remembered scraps.

The earth seems patched and stitched, like an old quilt
We gather in our sleep, its fields and folds
Shaped to our human contours. Dust and stone,
Grass, sand, and wooded hills, shift and erode,
Rise, settle, or sift away, depending on where
Time, love, or chance removes us. In our sleep
We first invade the new and make it our own.

So, dreaming, I first came here—these woods and hills,
Remembered or recovered more than found.
The signs and crowded streets of the known and near
Grew distant, as down winding roads I came
To this strange place half-fashioned from whole cloth
I rend by entering. . . .

            As if out of sleep
And woolly-eyed from dreaming, I came to
And found the world again—in one windfall,
Perspectives changed, as valley, lake, and hill
Baffle the breeze which stirs the shades, and now
Unfold against the slowly brightening window.

Crossing America by Bus

I
Past bums, past drunks, past con-men, beggars, and pimps
as permanent as pain, each at his station,
we enter the terminal. Though the law defines them
wishfully as *transients,* it is truly
we who, lumbering past them, are the transients,
heavy as beasts under our weight of luggage. . . .

Because there's something criminal about travel,
or a shade unsavory, like sex or death, that lures
the tourist, pilgrim, and escaping felon;
of both the murderer and saint, we say
they are *transported* out of the narrow country
of law to a New World, savage and mythical.

For what does travel tell us, but that we're mortal?
It's a short leap from *transit* to *transitory,*
which even Webster, stung into poetry,
defined as "fleeting," or "temporary,
as human life." And sea-tossed Odysseus,
his name become synonymous with journey,
knew that travail and travel had one root.

And yet, inert as freight, with the day's news
spread like a checkered cloth across our laps,
we abandon home and the medicine cabinet ·
face that greets us mornings, stow our worn luggage
with memory in the dark hold, and enter a bright future
with an innocence only distances will cure.

II
And distances are everywhere around us.

The days and nights, the mountains and the deserts—
and the small towns circumscribed by salt-flats, prairies,
badlands, buttes, plateaus, or surrounded by corn . . .
how the passing eye can size them up in a second
at a bus stop or gas station,
measure the workman's rounds
from rock quarry or grease pit
                              to the trailer around the corner,
or the waitress's glide
from table to kitchen to home to cemetery
at the town's sage-grown and dust-bitten edge.

        How easily the vagrant eye,
transcendent behind blue glass, and bloodshot from travel,
three days out from home in the air-conditioned cabin
and coming over the Alleghenies' green
into summery Pennsylvania
can expand to embrace the landscape, and the heart open
out and down into the dark earth, pillaged for iron,
or wide to the peopled, wild, or cattle and crop-bearing hills
till the body becomes light and sweet as a honeysuckle blossom,
shaking weariness off
the way a dog flings off the extra weight of water,
and pain and death evaporate in the soul's heat.

III
Then the bus stops. And the passengers jostle
toward the exit, stepping down
into heat and noise and the pain of missed connections.
Our luggage lost, we enter empty-handed
and swollen-footed, like Oedipus, into a strange city
with all the weight of time and distance on us
like a tragic curse, but which is merely
the condition we call human,
cured by a long sleep.

Which is another kind of travel.

Travellers in Space and Time

In 1969,
the year I graduated from high school,
Neil Armstrong and Colonel Edwin Aldrin
touched down
on the moon's then-virgin
Sea of Tranquility.
Their lunar module,
wrapped partly in gold foil,
now looks more like a piece of junkyard sculpture
than a likely umbilical
to the inevitable blue jewel
earth-rising, in the next picture,
above gray-brown moon swales
now glittery with the spacemen's picnic litter.
Their Moon Car,
or Lunar Roving Vehicle,
looks sand-colored, and functional
as a dune buggy
or a hot-rod chassis
to which two aluminum lawn chairs have been strapped;
instead of a steering wheel,
a kind of joy-stick stands erect
next to the right hand seat.
No windshield,
of course. Perhaps a battery
powers it, or
that thing in front
like an upturned umbrella
cocked like an ear toward space.

Impossible
that there are men inside those
inflatable white suits—
though in a parody
of our Pledge of Allegiance,
"Astronaut David Scott, of Apollo 15
salutes the American flag,"
his hand held to his black visor
the way a medieval knight
might have lifted his iron grillwork
in a similar gesture,
or, to be more up-to-date,
like Darth Vader
of the Star Wars trilogy.
The flag itself
is perpendicular
to the moon's surface,
as if it snapped and cracked
in a thirty-knot gale,
though then the footprints in the gray-green dust
would have been erased.

And turning the pages
of this month's book club paperback,
which are glossy and slick
as my high school yearbook, I see
a giant sheet metal silo

rising above the airless, cratered plain
of a more desolate Kansas
labelled, "An artist's impression
of a future lunar base,"
and near it an isolate spaceman hopping about
to whom I would like to affix the additional caption,
"Most Likely to Suffocate
Or Explode."

But now, instead, I ride
the author's hypothetical
beam of light
past Saturn
as easily as in my dream last night
I rode my high school bus
as it headed toward our twentieth reunion.
I remember cracking as the camera snapped
for our reunion picture,
"This can't be us—
we're twenty years too old!"
and then awakening
as my classmates' laughter died
to discover that that time
of which these lunar pictures might be emblems
is gone,
though, paradoxically,
somehow unchanged, still present,
my twentieth reunion four years off. . . .

As if,
Oh, Mercury
heart, on an earth grown
millenially older,
we might still return
twenty years later
by our interstellar clock,
after travelling at or near the speed of light,
to such millenial innocence again.

An American in Paris

Leaving behind your *Madame Bovary,*
Your *L'Education sentimental,*
Homer and Horace, and Latin elegy,
You dropped your books and left America
In headlong flight to Paris.
                          Why such haste?—
To tour old churches?
                          No. To speak a tongue
You'd only murmured formerly to ghosts?
To poke through ruins, to sight Mt. Helicon?
No, it wasn't art or literature you chased.
Skulking through streets, a rangy Baudelaire
From Berkeley, California, USA,
Your true Penelope was *not* Flaubert—
A young girl's arms was all your Ithaca. . . .
Soft eyes, soft laughter . . .
                          As the sun went down,
To earth and ocean, tangled in her hair,
You spoke her name, as old as Night and Sky—
Your *Phebe*, whom the poet called "gold-crowned."

Introduction to Poetry

She comes in late, then settles like a sigh
On the first day, returning every week
Promptly at ten, each Monday Wednesday Friday,
To study Shakespeare, Jonson, Donne, and Blake;

Enters the room to an approving murmur,
Straightens her dress, then, brushing back her hair,
Arches her body with the slightest tremor,
And sits, while the room grows breathless, in her chair;

Sits for an hour, while busy sophomores worry
Each turgid line, a Botticellian smile
On her rapt face, who's learned how little study
Love involves; who, walking down the aisle,

Knows in her bones how little poetry
Words breathe, and how—on turning to go home—
All eyes will watch her rise above her "C"
And walk off, like a goddess on the foam.

Strength

In grocery stores and discount supermarkets,
With names like *Flex* and *Strength*, on metal racks,
Where dodging husbands tag behind their wives
To finger them, the muscle magazines
Grow thicker and more brazen every year,
Like the trunks and limbs their pages advertise:

Half naked, bronzed, two smiling Amazons
Are twined and vined around a golden giant
More like the heroes in a comic book
Than someone that might stare back from a mirror.
With thighs "like tree trunks," biceps "big as boulders,"
He stares back from the page, as if to say,

"This could be you—this *should* be—if you weren't
The ninety-nine pound weakling that you are."
Rock hard and rubber-veined, his face a grimace,
He grunts and strains to keep that god-like poise.
Oiled and nearly hairless as a statue,
Hefting his lance, he'd seem a paragon,

If not so comic—as if Superman,
In cape and silly uniform had posed
For a Greek statue—say, the *Discobolus*,
Or, given the two girls, the *Laocoön*,
Trapped in the serpent's all-too-feminine coils.
This is the Hulk or Thing in all of us

Transformed. Between this month's *Good Housekeeping*
And *Modern Bride*, it beckons with its promise
Of perfect manhood, cured of fat and tanned
By pills, like those for impotence and baldness,
According to the back page classifieds,
Where books will tell you How to Pick Up Girls,

Or (for another fourteen ninety-five)
Tell how to make them sleep with you, or laugh.

An Apparition

Bent, cantilever, over a low drawer,
the full hips balance the swung breasts, catching
the lamplight's opalescent half-
crescent full on
one rondure.
                    Downed
        lightly, but gathered more full where
                shadow blends with curved shadow. . . .
                        the light fails—
a sight so tremulous
    and wearing no garment
but the half-light,
                no ornament
    but what the dark draws
    to it out of sister dark—
a shape that, flowing, moves
    as a shadow moves,
but embraced takes on such substance
    as a body fully nine-tenths water
                might take—
        moon pale, with a taste of ocean.

Concerning Angels: A Poetry Reading
for Robert Pinsky and Bob Hass

With the crayon-bright
colors of children's books
and Christmas calendars
behind him on the shelf,
the poet reads
about a girl sitting in
a garden, reading letters by moonlight;
and because she is alone
in the dark
among stunted trees, and white-faced
as the moon she's reading by,
reader and listener
know that the woman burns
in the white, blue,
or red flames of
desire.

Desire,
that Christmas angel
with gilded wings!
Who has not seen her, blonde
and unreachable atop
her pinnacle of lights
and tinsel, or bedizened
on any neon-blazoned
red light district street,
and not felt all desire
merely childish—
like painted gold leaf,
whose glitter stains the thumb.

But now, as the poet reads
and the spotlight folds a rainbow
of colors behind him,
we abandon ourselves to the
implausible
dragons and circumstances
of the childish fictions
of poems,
recognizing in them something
like an answer to our need. . . .
Read me a story
we say, because
after the father's voice
stops, and the lamplight
goes out, there is only
dark, cold, and the fading
warmth of another's body
beside us; because only
words can fill that gap
between one dark
and the next, their
once upon a time
lending a shape to desire.

So, as the garish,
candy-colored
monsters and unicorns
of dreams
replace the Fauvist
paradisal islands
and green tropics
that illustrate this earth,
we allow the names of things
to linger happily
in mind, saying *moon,*
woman, letter, poem, angel—
letting their echoes sound
that dark beyond
desire, like pennies falling
into the blue depths
of a wishing well.

Summer Revisited

Summer arrives, and the air is
humid with memories
of a simpler existence—
as if all summers
were one
summer, broken
by cold
snaps, spring's
resurrections, heavy
with the accumulation
of time—merely
pushed aside, rather than cut through.

All is lush, with a greenhouse denseness.
Like an approaching storm,
time gathers, thickening the air,
and like all the storms we watched from our country house,
this storm threatens
with a pending fury.

Let the lightning flash
that would split this tension!
Let the rain fall
smack on the trees,
banging the leaves like cymbals.

After the first discharge
of light,
there comes a stillness
where the rain stops
and the sky takes in its breath,

where for one moment, nature seems suspended
above its laws,
and the seconds hang
like flung gravel in midair. . . .

*   *   *

On a back road
heavy with dust
under an August sun
I shoveled gravel,
pitching and scattering
the dusty stone
over hot tar
off a slow truck.
There was a point
where the stones paused
weightless in their arch
(you could have counted them)
before falling, and
by flinging my shovel
hard into the pile
and like a paddle pitching
them out, out,
out, there was
a continuous galaxy
of them hanging there,
the sum of several
motions, caught
in a motionless instant.

*   *   *

But time is a storm
and after its eye passes
the merciless seconds
are blown in our eyes
like fine dust off stone
and no amount of weeping
can clear them from our vision.
We must console ourselves
with remembered time,

with remembered summers:
how their moments hang
clumped like ripe berries in thickets!

                *   *   *

In the smouldering field
in August heat,
I stood guard over
the circling forest,
a five-gallon water can
strapped to my back,
and in my hand
a small pump
that arched a thin stream
of unpotable water
hissing over the live coals
of trash and tree stumps.

65

And then to discover them
in the half light
at the field's perimeter
under their coat of dust
and smoke ash: raspberries,
plump and ripe and heavy on the branch
with their weight of sweetness!

In the shade I ate them
till I could eat no more.

And having stripped
but a small part
of a hundred bushes,
I thought: there is a kind of joy
can only be borne in measures,
as if by accident,
looking up from the day's task—
a kind of surfeit
of sweetness
from which we must retire,
at length, back into the haze
of summer heat—

returned to only
in dreams and memory—

though the shade beckons
to deeper shade
whispering *raspberries,*
raspberries.